EAT LIKE A LOCAL
BOOK SERIES REVIEWS

Eat Like a Local- Sarasota: Sarasota Florida Food Guide

I have lived in the Sarasota area since 1998 and learned about many great places that I want to try. –Conoal

EAT LIKE A LOCAL-CONNECTICUT: Connecticut Food Guide

This a great guide to try different places in Connecticut to eat. Can't wait to try them all! The author is awesome to explore and try all these different foods/drinks. There are places I didn't know they existed until I got this book and I am a CT resident myself! –Caroline J. H.

EAT LIKE A LOCAL- LAS VEGAS: Las Vegas Nevada Food Guide

Perfect food guide for any tourist traveling to Vegas or any local looking to go outside their comfort zone! –TheBondes

Eat Like a Local-Jacksonville: Jacksonville Florida Food Guide

Loved the recommendations. Great book from someone who knows their way around Jacksonville. –Anonymous

EAT LIKE A LOCAL- COSTA BRAVA: Costa Brava Spain Food Guide

The book was very well written. Visited a few of the restaurants in the book, they were great! Sylvia V.

Eat Like a Local-Sacramento: Sacramento California Food Guide

As a native of Sacramento, Emerald's book touches on some of our areas premier spots for food and fun. She skims the surface of what Sacramento has to offer recommending locations in historical, popular areas where even more jewels can be found. –Katherine G.

EAT LIKE A LOCAL- ST. LOUIS

St. Louis Missouri Food Guide

Erin Robbins

Eat Like a Local- St. Louis Copyright © 2022 by CZYK Publishing LLC. All Rights Reserved.

This book contains information about alcohol.

All rights reserved. No part of this book may be reproduced in any form or by any electronic or mechanical means including information storage and retrieval systems, without permission in writing from the author. The only exception is by a reviewer, who may quote short excerpts in a review.

The statements in this book are of the authors and may not be the views of CZYK Publishing.

Cover designed by: Lisa Rusczyk Ed. D.

CZYK Publishing Since 2011.

CZYKPublishing.com

Eat Like a Local

Mill Hall, PA

All rights reserved.

ISBN: 9798826043578

BOOK DESCRIPTION

Are you excited about planning your next trip? Do you want an edible experience? Would you like some culinary guidance from a local? If you answered yes to any of these questions, then this Eat Like a Local book is for you. Eat Like a Local - St. Louis by Erin Robbins offers the inside scoop on food in St. Louis. Culinary tourism is an important aspect of any travel experience. Food has the ability to tell you a story of a destination, its landscapes, and culture on a single plate. Most food guides tell you how to eat like a tourist. Although there is nothing wrong with that, as part of the Eat Like a Local series, this book will give you a food guide from someone who has lived at your next culinary destination.

In these pages, you will discover advice on having a unique edible experience. This book will not tell you exact addresses or hours but instead will give you excitement and knowledge of food and drinks from a local that you may not find in other travel food guides.

Eat like a local. Slow down, stay in one place, and get to know the food, people, and culture. By the time you finish this book, you will be eager and prepared to travel to your next culinary destination.

OUR STORY

Traveling has always been a passion of the creator of the Eat Like a Local book series. During Lisa's travels in Malta, instead of tasting what the city offered, she ate at a large fast-food chain. However, she realized that her traveling experience would have been more fulfilling if she had experienced the best of local cuisines. Most would agree that food is one of the most important aspects of a culture. Through her travels, Lisa learned how much locals had to share with tourists, especially about food. Lisa created the Eat Like a Local book series to help connect people with locals which she discovered is a topic that locals are very passionate about sharing. So please join me and: Eat, drink, and explore like a local.

TABLE OF CONTENTS

Eat Like a Local-
Book Series Reviews
BOOK DESCRIPTION
OUR STORY
TABLE OF CONTENTS
DEDICATION
ABOUT THE AUTHOR
HOW TO USE THIS BOOK
FROM THE PUBLISHER
1. Getting There And Getting Around
2. How To Pay
3. The Etiquette Of Tips
4. To Read Or Not To Read
5. When To Eat
6. Happy, Happy Hours
7. Go Nuts For Donuts
8. Eggcelent
9. Did Somebody Say "Mimosas?"
10. Delicatessen Delight
11. Dinner Or Supper?
12. Nicer Than Normal
13. Fine Dining
14. As American As Blueberry Pie
15. Root Beer And A Restaurant

16. The All American Burger Joint
17. Let's Taco Bout It
18. Pita Party Time
19. Who Doesn't Love An Irish pub?
20. On The Hill
21. Off the Hill
22. The Square Beyond Compare
23. No, We're The Best
24. Okay, But Where Do I Get It?
25. Food "Trucks"
26. Meat Me In St. Louie
27. No Meat For Me
28. Vegan, Please
29. Going Against The Grain
30. Nectar Of The Gods
31. The Great St. Louis Bake Off
32. Now Make It Gluten Free
33. Like Cake, But Smaller
34. Like A Kid In A Candy Shop
35. We All Scream For Ice Cream!
36. We All Scream For No Cream
37. We All Scream for…Gelato!
38. Wine A Little
39. Brew Can Do It!
40. The King Of Beers
41. Cheers!

42. ↑ ↑ ↓ ↓ ← → ← → B A Start
43. The Puzzle Bar
44. Nights Out
45. What A Drag
46. Calling All Sports Fans
47. QuikTrip
48. Grocery stores
49. Ravioli, But Toasted
50. Last, But Absolutely Not Least

Bonus Tip #1

Bonus Tip #2

Bonus Tip #3

READ OTHER BOOKS BY
CZYK PUBLISHING

DEDICATION

This book is dedicated to my husband, Garrett. Thank you for always encouraging me to take risks and to shoot the big shots. I'd also like to thank my mom, Ronda, for introducing me to so many of these amazing restaurants. Thank you both for years of love and support.

ABOUT THE AUTHOR

Erin is someone who has always loved to travel, and has found every excuse to do just that. She also loves to share her adventures with whoever will listen. Having been to 19 countries, and all over the US, Erin loves to be immersed in other cultures (eating is probably her favorite way to do this). She has always believed that the more you travel, the better of a person you are. The more of the world you see, the more you see the lives of other people, the more likely you are to be sympathetic to the people around you. At the end of every trip though, she is always excited to come home, mostly so she can start planning her next trip.

When not traveling, Erin loves to express her creativity with painting, knitting, and embroidering. She also loves to explore the creativity of others by reading every book she can get her hands on. Or, you know, just rereading the same three fantasy series over and over again. Usually though, she can be found in one coffee shop or another sipping on Americanos and cold brew.

These days, Erin lives in southern California with her husband and two cats and is probably reading on the beach as you read this. Having had to move away from St. Louis for work, Erin is always excited to get to go home. Mostly to get to eat gooey butter cake and drink Fitz's, but seeing her family and the city is fun too. To quote Nelly, one of the more famous people to come out of St. Louis this century, Erin says, "I'm from the Lou and I'm proud!"

HOW TO USE THIS BOOK

The goal of this book is to help culinary travelers either dream or experience different edible experiences by providing opinions from a local. The author has made suggestions based on their own knowledge. Please do your own research before traveling to the area in case the suggested locations are unavailable.

Travel Advisories: As a first step in planning any trip abroad, check the Travel Advisories for your intended destination.
https://travel.state.gov/content/travel/en/traveladvisories/traveladvisories.html

FROM THE PUBLISHER

Traveling can be one of the most important parts of a person's life. The anticipation and memories that you have are some of the best. As a publisher of the *Eat Like a Local*, Greater Than a Tourist, as well as the popular *50 Things to Know* book series, we strive to help you learn about new places, spark your imagination, and inspire you. Wherever you are and whatever you do I wish you safe, fun, and inspiring travel.

Lisa Rusczyk Ed. D.
CZYK Publishing

Eat Like a Local

"Food brings people together on many different levels. It's nourishment of the soul and body; it's truly love."

– *Giada De Laurentiis*

No matter where in the world I may wander, I'm always glad to be able to come back home. For me, home is St. Louis, Missouri, The Gateway to the West. It's a place I love and am glad to have grown up. We have a busy and full history that spans back to pre-Columbian times, and that has influenced the city to be the unique and diverse place it is today. At various points in time, we were the largest Native American trading hub north of Mexico, a Spanish settlement, a French settlement, a part of the Louisiana Purchase, and the starting point for settlers to head West. With all of these different cultures interacting and mingling, it is no wonder that St. Louis is a very diverse and international city today.

We have been the location of many important events in history. St. Louis was the place of the historic Dred Scott Case, and the site of a Revolutionary War battle. The confluence of the two rivers was the start of the Lewis and Clark expedition, and a century later, the city hosted a world's fair and the Olympics in honor of that important event. We are the birthplace of countless celebrities such as Maya Angelou, Chuck Berry, and Josephine Baker, and more recently Jenna Fischer, John Hamm, and Andy Cohen.

Today, St. Louis is a booming metropolis in the center of the United States. The populace is diverse, with people coming here from all over the country and world to live here. We are the home of two popular and successful sports teams, the Cardinals and Blues. We have a zoo that is widely regarded as one of the best zoos in the world and it's free. Speaking of free, we also have free museums and theater, and one of the largest urban parks in the country. Most notably, we are the home to the Gateway Arch. The tallest monument in America, the Arch is the symbol of the city.

Eat Like a Local

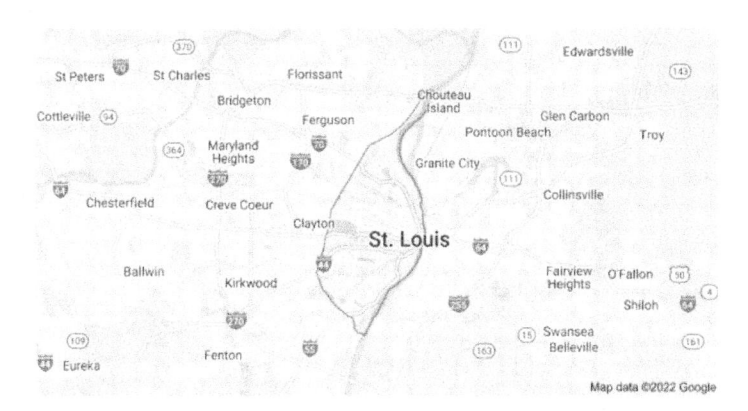

St. Louis
Missouri, USA

St. Louis Missouri Climate

	High	Low
January	40	23
February	45	27
March	56	38
April	67	48
May	77	58
June	86	67
July	90	71
August	88	69
September	81	61
October	70	50
November	57	39
December	44	29

GreaterThanaTourist.com

Temperatures are in Fahrenheit degrees.
Source: NOAA

1. GETTING THERE AND GETTING AROUND

So I've convinced you to come to St. Louis, where is it? We are in the Midwest, the heart of America. More specifically, we're on the eastern edge of Missouri, right where the Mississippi and Missouri Rivers meet. So how do you get here? We have an international airport that you can fly into, or, you can do the more Midwestern thing, and take a road trip to us. (Seriously, road trips are kind of a Midwestern specialty. It's 12 hours away? Doesn't matter, we're driving and stopping at every World's Largest Rubber Band Ball along the way.) Thankfully, we're easy to drive to on account of there being four major interstates that pass through.

Now you've gotten here, yay! Now what, do you need a car? Most likely the answer to that is a strong yes. While we do have a bus and public transit system, it has a pretty limited reach and I wouldn't exactly call it reliable. If you plan on staying in a small radius downtown, you would be fine with just walking and taking Ubers, Lyfts, and taxis. However, if you want to go further than a couple of miles, I strongly recommend renting a car. It gives you much more freedom to go where you want, when you want.

Now, there's just one more thing you need to know before you venture out to explore to your stomach's content, and that is that there are two counties in Missouri called St. Louis. I know, not confusing at all. There's St. Louis City (which most of us just call downtown), and St. Louis County (the suburbs). Many of these recommendations are specifically for the City, as that's where people generally stay when they come to visit. However, I did include several options for St. Louis County (and even a couple for the country after that, St. Charles.) Don't worry though, because of the aforementioned four major interstates, nothing is much further than 20 minutes away. Of the few recommendations that are further, I made sure to include that in the description so you can decide for yourself if you want to make the drive.

2. HOW TO PAY

Nearly every store and restaurant will take both credit/debit cards and cash. There will be the occasional place that doesn't take one or the other, but they are few and far between. What you might have more issues finding is contactless payment. While it has gotten more popular in recent years, it still is not popular enough of a function to be able to expect places to have.

3. THE ETIQUETTE OF TIPS

Tipping is ingrained in many parts of American culture. It isn't some grand statement you make when you don't tip, it just hurts the people serving you. While other industries can also expect a tip at the end of service, it is most common in the food industry. Here is a general guide for the minimum recommended tips:

Full service restaurant: 15-20%

Buffet: 10%

Baristas: $1/drink OR 15% if your bill also includes food

Bartenders: $1-2/drink OR 15% if your bill also includes food

4. TO READ OR NOT TO READ

Many times before trying out a new restaurant, I'll check the internet to see what other people have said about it. Online reviews can be a double edged sword though. They can be well written and informed, or they could be influenced by one angry person. Regardless, it's always a good idea to check the recent reviews on multiple websites to see if a particular restaurant is what you're wanting that day.

I also like to look up a restaurant on Instagram. This gives me an idea of what the portion sizes will look like and gives me an idea of what the expected attire is. Plus, who doesn't like to look at beautiful photos of delicious food?

5. WHEN TO EAT

It's hard to recommend a good time to eat when each person will have a different idea of what works best for them. It really comes down to your preferences and your plans for the day, just be aware that certain times will be busier than others. If you're spending time downtown during the week, lunch hour picks up but doesn't normally get particularly crazy, especially at a sit-down restaurant. Most office workers will go somewhere with quick service so that they can get in and out and back to work. Weekends though, can be pretty busy, expect a 30+ minute wait during normal meal times. You can expect that to be even longer if you are near the stadiums during games or near a theater house before a show.

6. HAPPY, HAPPY HOURS

If you're not picky about the time you want to go out and want to save a couple dollars, be on the lookout for happy hours. Most will be off peak hours, but are well worth the trip out for the savings to be had. Many bars and restaurants have some sort of deal on drinks at some point in the day, though often between the lunch and dinner crowds. The restaurant might offer deals on specific drinks only, or it could be a flat rate discount. Oftentimes, specific food items are also included in these deals.

7. GO NUTS FOR DONUTS

Looking for a quick and sweet breakfast? St. Louis has a surprising amount of donut shops that might pique your interests. There are two shops in particular that stand out from the rest. First, is Old Town Donuts in Florissant. If you want the best classic style donuts, this is the place to go. On top of donuts, they also offer a small selection of other pastries, and don't get me wrong, those are good too, but the donuts are the real stars of the show. They are also open 24 hours, so if you have a hankering for something sweet after a night out, this is a great place to go.

The second donut shop is something a little…different. One might even call it strange. From flavors like maple bacon to pina colada to rainbow pony, there is something for every taste bud at Strange Donuts. They close at noon, though, so get there early to make sure you get one (or two, or three) of these cakey flakey donuts.

8. EGGCELENT

If your accommodations don't offer a free breakfast (or, let's be real, you're tired of the same powdered eggs you've had every morning), there are plenty of amazing breakfast joints in St. Louis. If you like eccentric and eclectic (and I mean those terms in the very best way) decor and vibes, the Mudhouse is the spot for you. Offering bottomless house coffee, vegan, vegetarian, and gluten free food options, and a cozy patio, The Mudhouse is a perfect local cafe.

If you're looking for something a bit more classic-American-Diner style, though, Uncle Bill's Pancake House is the best. Open 24 hours a day, it's almost more common to go here after a long night out than it is for breakfast. (At least that was the case in my college days.) Whenever you decide to visit, the pancakes are always to die for.

9. DID SOMEBODY SAY "MIMOSAS?"

Like many other large cities, St. Louis has caught on to the brunch craze and it doesn't look like we're letting go anytime soon. Something about day drinking and eating enough for the whole day in one meal has us hooked. The best spot for a casual and relaxed brunch is The Shack. There are several locations in and around the city, each with quirky and unique decor. Be sure to bring your sharpie so you can add your name to the walls, which are covered in names and dates of previous guests! In addition to the normal food, The Shack offers a way to modify much of the menu to be gluten free, and vegetarian.

10. DELICATESSEN DELIGHT

For a quick lunch that isn't a chain fast food spot, check out one of the many local delis. The best spot to find a guaranteed good sandwich is the local Little Italy neighborhood called The Hill. More on that area later, though. For my favorite deli, you have to go a little ways out of St. Louis proper, and into the neighboring county of St. Charles. Located on historic Main Street (which is a wonderful little

Eat Like a Local

shopping area) is a small deli called Valenti's. They have both standard and unique sandwiches at an affordable price. If it's in season, I highly recommend the lobster reuben. They also offer catering services if you'll be in town for a large gathering.

11. DINNER OR SUPPER?

Whatever it is you call the meal that takes place in the evenings, the Midwest is different from many other places as we eat fairly early, this is especially true for families with younger kids. That said, most St. Louis dinner spots will start to get busy from 5:30 and stay that way for several hours until typically dying off around 8 or 8:30 and will probably close shortly after at 9. The exceptions to this would be restaurants that have more of a bar feel, and those are more likely to get busy a little later and stay open until 11.

12. NICER THAN NORMAL

Sometimes you're in the mood for something nicer than your average dinner, but still not quite fine dining. While St. Louis has plenty of restaurants that fit that bill, I cannot recommend Polite Society enough. Perfect for a semi formal occasion like an anniversary for a young couple, Polite Society has a seasonal food and cocktail menu. Located in historic Lafayette Square, you know you're in a nicer area than normal just by the surrounding buildings. Despite the seasonal menu, it is easy to get information on any of the dishes, as the staff is highly trained to help you with allergies and preferences. While not required to make a reservation, I do suggest doing so, especially if you plan on visiting on the weekend.

13. FINE DINING

If, though, something only a little nicer than normal won't do, St. Louis does have some fine dining experiences for you. Like all fine dining establishments, reservations are recommended for all visits, even during the week. We might not have any Michelin stars, but we do have several restaurants around the city and county that have been recognized by the James Beard Award. One of these is Little Fox. This hip establishment may not be what you immediately think of when you think of fine dining, but the food here speaks for itself. Little Fox is known for the concept of serving many small plates for sharing with only one or two large entrees for the whole table. Being a fine dining establishment, the cost will be higher than your average meal, but that price is well worth the experience of eating at such a nice restaurant.

14. AS AMERICAN AS BLUEBERRY PIE

Yes, I know the saying is "as American as apple pie," but the restaurant with the best American cuisine in St. Louis isn't called Apple Hill, it's Blueberry Hill. Located on the Delmar Loop, a popular eating and shopping district with college age folks, Blueberry Hill is one of the most St. Louis restaurants in St. Louis. If that made sense. In addition to being an affordable food option, the restaurant doubles as an intimate concert venue that has hosted the likes of Chuck Berry. From the food to decor, they balance nostalgia from all eras of American history while also firmly embracing the modern day.

15. ROOT BEER AND A RESTAURANT

Ask anyone from St. Louis to pick a favorite soda, and chances are that most of us will say Fitz's. One thing that differentiates this root beer from many other sodas is the old school practice of using cane sugar instead of high fructose corn syrup. I don't know if it's the glass bottle, the natural ingredients, or just the fact that it calls St. Louis home, but I will die on the hill that Fitz's is the best root beer in the world.

Though it can be found all over the city, the best way to experience Ftiz's is to go to the Loop and visit the restaurant. There, you can see the original bottling machine and get bottomless mugs of this delicious drink. If you don't want root beer, you can also try one of their many other flavors of soda. Whatever you decide, come thirsty, come hungry, and let Fitz's fill you up.

16. THE ALL AMERICAN BURGER JOINT

There's nothing much more traditionally American than a burger and a milkshake. To get this great experience, pop in to one of several Hi-Pointe Drive-In's. With the option for veggie burgers and gluten free buns, there's a burger here for everyone.

If what you're looking for is some great sides to accompany your burger, Stacked Burger Bar is the restaurant for you. The burgers here all have punny names and taste great, but the sides. The sides and starters here are some of the best I've ever had and there is as wide a variety of these as there are burger options.

17. LET'S TACO BOUT IT

There are so many amazing Mexican restaurants in St. Louis, it is hard to recommend only one. Some are traditional Mexican, others have a Tex-Mex spin on them, and others still base their identity on the street taco. That last option in particular has come to be quite popular among the younger generations. A chain that has come up in the last decade or so that really shows that is Mission Taco Joint. The owners grew up in southern California eating Mexican street food. They brought these flavors to St. Louis and opened their first restaurant. Now there are several locations throughout the city (with a great late night happy hour, I might add).

18. PITA PARTY TIME

As I've already mentioned, there is a large international presence in St. Louis. A large number of current immigrants are coming to us from the Mediterranean, bringing with them their cultures and food. A newer restaurant that I love is off the beaten path for most tourists, but Kaslik Mediterranean Cuisine is worth the journey out of St. Louis City and into St. Louis County.

Kaslik, relatively new compared to most of the other restaurants on this list, serves up a variety of Mediterranean and Middle Eastern dishes. One important thing to note: don't expect traditional, over attentive, American service when you come here.

19. WHO DOESN'T LOVE AN IRISH PUB?

I'm not going to lie, sometimes when I'm traveling I don't want to try something new, I just want something I know. That doesn't mean I want to go to a big, national chain, I just want some food that I get exactly what I'm expecting. My favorite way to achieve that is to find a local Irish pub; it's food that I know I'll love but is prepared with just a slightly different recipe than what I've had anywhere else.

While my favorite pub in St. Louis does happen to be a chain, it's a chain that is native to St. Louis. Llywelyn's Pub (okay, okay, so this was technically a Welsh pub, but the menu was expanded to embrace Irish and Scottish fare) has several locations around the city, and pours the best Guiness around.

20. ON THE HILL

St. Louis is made up of dozens of small neighborhoods, one of the most famous of those is the Hill. The Hill is a downtown area that is now made up of largely Italian immigrants who settled in St. Louis in the early 1900s. When it was founded, the Hill was

Eat Like a Local

made up of Irish and German immigrants who were trying to make ends meet at the nearby trainyard. Today, though, the area is distinctly Italian. They embrace the Italian culture and history and are extremely proud of their heritage.

The Hill is home to dozens of traditional Italian markets, delis, and restaurants. From Adriana's to Zia's, any place you choose to eat at on The Hill will easily be the best Italian food you'll ever eat outside Italy. I may even go so far as to say it's the consistently best food in the city, period.

21. OFF THE HILL

Don't let that last tip fool you, The Hill isn't the only place to go in St. Louis for some great Italian food. There are plenty of options all over the city. However, if you feel like venturing out of the city and into the more residential county, you will find a couple of my favorite restaurants, Nick and Elena's Pizzeria, and Serra's Pizzeria. Over the years, both stores have had to add expansions to their buildings to be able to accommodate more guests; even with these add ons, they are always packed.

Both are family owned and operated and serve up traditional Italian and Sicilian food, and everything is made in house. Nick and Elena's has a disclaimer printed on all the menus that says, "There are <u>real</u> Italians working in this kitchen, at any time you may observe yelling, kicking, screaming, biting, and various other activities associated with Italian cooking. So sit back and enjoy!" On my many visits to the store, I can attest that the warning is appreciated and needed; but, hey, it only adds to the atmosphere of a family owned Italian restaurant.

22. THE SQUARE BEYOND COMPARE

When I say pizza, square probably isn't the shape you think of. St. Louis style pizza, though, is famous for being cut into square pieces. Other than shape, what makes our pizza unique is its oh-so-thin crust and provel cheese topping rather than mozzarella.

The most famous example of St. Louis pizza can be found at a chain of restaurants called Imo's Pizza. Easily the most popular pizza delivery in the area, Imo's prides itself on serving other popular St. Louis specific dishes as well, most notably toasted ravioli

Eat Like a Local

(don't worry, there will be more on this particular dish later).

On the chance you're thinking "thin crust? No, give me a deep dish," then Pi Pizzeria is the place for you. While they do offer some traditional St. Louis style pizzas, they also have quite a bit that is less traditional. Be sure to not confuse "less traditional" with "unpopular," this shop has garnered such a positive reputation that the owner was flown from St. Louis to visit the White House and cook for the Obama Administration in 2014! The menu at Pi has pizzas named after St. Louis neighborhoods, and the beers on tap are brewed locally. Ensuring that, even if the food isn't all done in a traditional style, you remember that you're in The Lou.

23. NO, WE'RE THE BEST

Wherever you go in the Midwest, every city claims to have the best bar-b-que in the world, and they're all wrong. Obviously, the award for best BBQ goes to St. Louis. What makes our BBQ different from other places that are famous for it? The main difference is the cooking time. Most other cities will slow cook their ribs for several hours before serving, whereas St. Louis is more likely to just grill them. Before grilling, the ribs are often coated with brown mustard and a dry spice rub and left to marinate for up to a full day. Then the ribs are put on a smokey grill. With just a little bit of time left in the smoker, we add the first layer of sweet and tangy St. Louis BBQ sauce, and when done cooking, we drench them in some more sauce.

24. OKAY, BUT WHERE DO I GET IT?

One of the best examples of St. Louis bar-b-que is a local chain called Sugarfire. What started as a local, single location, restaurant and has grown to have 15 locations across 6 states. They have won countless awards and titles and have been featured on shows like Pitmasters. Another popular location for St. Louis BBQ is Salt + Smoke, which pairs bar-b-que with beer and bourbon. It is also unique in that they don't add that last layer of sauce, instead, there are a variety of sauces at your table for you to add as much or as little as you would like.

Eat Like a Local

25. FOOD "TRUCKS"

Remember the food truck fad of the 2010s? Yeah, St. Louis hasn't been ready to let go of that yet. There are still several very popular and successful food trucks operating in the area. One of the most beloved is Mann Meats. While it may sound like something an orc would like and isn't technically a food *truck* (it operates out of an old converted school bus), Mann Meats is another home to some great St. Louis bar-b-que. Every morning they send out a Facebook post and tweet with their location and stay there until a specified time or they sell out. They very rarely make it to that specified time. If you don't feel like hunting down a restaurant that moves every day, they now have a brick and mortar location in St. Louis County with the same delicious food as the food truck. Be warned, the store operates on the same motto of "until X o'clock or sell out," so you may want to consider this for lunch rather than dinner.

26. MEAT ME IN ST. LOUIE

The Midwest is home to the "meat and potatoes" mindset that much American Cuisine is known for, and it is easy to find that sort of meal at most restaurants. However, if you're specifically looking for a good cut of steak, that might be hard to find at your average restaurant. Luckily, there are plenty of steakhouses to choose from in the area.

One of the nicer, and more popular, of these is The Tenderloin Room. Located in the Chase Park Plaza, one of the nicer hotels in the area, in the heart of the Central West End, the Tenderloin Room is a great spot for a nice anniversary dinner. It is one of the higher end restaurants in this guide, so be sure to book a reservation in advance.

27. NO MEAT FOR ME

As with most major cities, St. Louis has many residents that choose to be meat free. While most restaurants have vegetarian items on the menu, it is often the case that you have to customize existing items to fit your needs. However, there are plenty of times you just don't want to worry about what you order. In times like that, be sure to check out Small

Batch. This completely meat free establishment has a seasonal menu of both vegetarian and vegan items, along with an expansive whiskey and cocktail menu.

28. VEGAN, PLEASE

Along with vegetarianism, veganism is on the rise and more popular than ever. That doesn't mean it's easy to find good food you know you can eat while you're out. There are a couple of local restaurants trying to remedy that that offer fully vegetarian and vegan kitchens. One such of these restaurants is Bombay Food Junkies. They are a vegan store that specializes in Indian street food. What started as a vegetarian food truck has already outgrown one brick and mortar location and moved into another. This extra space has also allowed for the menu to be shifted to a fully vegan menu, to the delight of many of the restaurant's fans.

29. GOING AGAINST THE GRAIN

Despite more and more people either being diagnosed with gluten intolerances or going gluten free by choice, there really aren't many dedicated gluten free places in St. Louis. While that may be the case, there are many places that are knowledgeable and understanding of cross contamination. If you want to comfortably eat dinner somewhere, I have to recommend The Corner Pub and Grill. While this is not a fully gluten free environment, the staff is highly trained on gluten intolerance and Celiac Disease and is fantastic about avoiding cross contamination. Owned by the same people that own The Shack, it shares that same quirky style. The biggest downside to this place is that it isn't downtown, but is about 30 minutes into the suburbs.

30. NECTAR OF THE GODS

To translate this title, coffee, beautiful coffee. When people think about cities known for coffee, St. Louis likely isn't on that list. While it might not be something we're known for, we do have a booming coffee scene. Regardless of the type of cafe you're

Eat Like a Local

looking for, chances are good that we have it. Whether you want a traditional Italian cafe, a new age coffee house, or a cat cafe, St. Louis has you covered.

All that said, my all time favorite cafe has to be Picasso's Coffee House. Located about 30 minutes outside of St. Louis City and in historic St. Charles, Picasso's is an art themed cafe with drinks to satisfy both the coffee snobs and those with a sweet tooth alike. Add in their signature cocktails and small food menu, it truly doesn't get much better than this place.

However, if you don't feel like leaving the city, swing by one of Blueprint Coffee's three locations downtown. This shop is a more traditional style, serving primarily espresso forward drinks and fewer milk based drinks. Despite this traditional approach, I have never felt like the employees here are snobbish at all, they always take the time to explain any questions I have had or heard. If you're interested in coffee at all, definitely try to make it to one of the cuppings they host!

31. THE GREAT ST. LOUIS BAKE OFF

I firmly stand by the fact that there's no such thing as a bad bakery. They are all wonderful because bakeries all produce cakes and tarts and scones. Although St. Louis has many, many delightful patisserie shops, one in particular stands out. La Bonne Bouchée, an authentic French patisserie and cafe. In addition to their mouth watering sweet treats, it has a small restaurant inside it that serves a small breakfast and lunch menu. Mostly, though, locals know La Bonne for its tasty sweet treats. In fact, many metro area coffee shops and cafes get daily pastry deliveries from La Bonne, ensuring that even people outside the city are able to enjoy their treats.

32. NOW MAKE IT GLUTEN FREE

If for whatever reason, you don't eat gluten but you still want delicious pastries, you're in luck! Britt's Bakehouse is here for you! This patisserie is fully gluten free and celiac safe, and many of the desserts have the option to be dairy or egg free. Every day they have a rotating and wide variety of tasty cupcakes, cookies, donuts, and more. Britt also offers customizable tiered cakes and take n' bake options. After discovering this gem, it quickly became one of my favorites, so much so that they provided desserts at my wedding!

33. LIKE CAKE, BUT SMALLER

If you're in the mood specifically for a cupcake, you have a surprising amount of options in St. Louis. On top of being the biggest cupcakes around, my all time favorite spot for a cupcake is Jilly's. Don't just take my word for it, Jilly's Cupcakes has received recognition from all over the country. Since being founded in 2007, they have competed on the Food Network show Cupcake Wars (and won twice!), been listed as one of the top ten places in the country to get a cupcake by USA Today, and been ranked seventh best cupcake in the nation by the Daily Meal Food Blog. On top of the consistent flavors that don't change, there are monthly flavors and boozy options to choose from!

34. LIKE A KID IN A CANDY SHOP

Sometimes you want something sweet, but a pastry just isn't what you're craving. For times like that, I like to go to Crown Candy Kitchen. One of the last candy stores of its era, walking into Crown Candy is like stepping back in time. All of the candy made in house is done so in the same method as it was 100 years ago by the current owner's grandfather. With a vintage jukebox in the corner and the oldest soda fountain in St. Louis, you can tell that this place has seen some history. In addition to the homemade candy (because nobody is leaving with no candy), you can pick up a quick lunch or dinner to take home with you. Crown Candy Kitchen is one of the true St. Louis staples that everyone that comes to the city needs to go to.

35. WE ALL SCREAM FOR ICE CREAM!

St. Louis might be a city with many thoughts and opinions on every topic imaginable, but there is one thing that we all agree on. That one thing is that Ted Drewes frozen custard is the best ice cream* in the city. Ted Drewes is the perfect end to a summer day spent downtown at the Arch and a Cardinal's game. This frozen treat isn't just for the hot summer days though; it is the perfect accompaniment to looking at the impressive Christmas light displays on Candy Cane Lane, located just around the corner. Rain, shine, or snow, there is always a crowd waiting for a world famous concrete to be served upside down. With their flagship location on historic Route 66, it is worth a visit for more than one reason. (*Yes, I am aware that frozen custard isn't technically ice cream, but this stuff is so good that I am more than happy to overlook that fact.)

36. WE ALL SCREAM FOR NO CREAM

If for some reason dairy isn't your thing, fret not! St. Louis has options! My favorite place to get a dairy free frozen treat is Ices Plain and Fancy. Unfortunately, it is not a fully vegan store, so there is always the risk of cross contamination, but the employees have always been happy to do a little extra when I have been there. What makes Ices special is their way of freezing the cream. Rather than use a slow churn method that is most common, Ices flash freezes it with liquid nitrogen, this gives it an even smoother feel than regular ice cream. In addition to the several vegan flavors, they also offer some boozy ice cream flavors.

Eat Like a Local

37. WE ALL SCREAM FOR...GELATO!

In addition to the many ice cream and frozen custard shops around, St. Louis has several options for gelato if you're wanting something a little different. The spot I have found with the best options available is The Gelateria Coffee Company in the Tower Grove neighborhood. Their name should make it pretty clear what their focus is, good gelato and good coffee. Even though they sit on a busy street, they manage to have a quiet and peaceful patio that is perfect for reading.

38. WINE A LITTLE

Say you want some high quality wine, you'll probably have to go to Napa or the European countryside, right? Wrong. If you drive just an hour or two outside of St. Louis, you will find some amazing local wineries. The land surrounding St. Louis is perfect for vineyards and we have taken great aadvantage of that. There are dozens of scenic small towns dotted along the Missouri River with their own wineries. You can also cross the Mighty Mississippi River and go into Illinois to find even more. One popular fall St. Louis activity is to take a whole day and follow the wine trail through the countryside from winery to winery, soaking in the scenery and tasting the many varieties of wine.

39. BREW CAN DO IT!

As great as our wine is, wine isn't everyone's thing. If that's the case, there are still plenty of local drinking options for you. St. Louis is home to many microbreweries and larger producers. The most well known of these breweries is Schlafly, which has grown from a small, one building operation, to a large scale company that services countless bars and grocery stores in St. Louis and beyond. Swing by one of their many taprooms and restaurants to get a tour and a taste.

If you're wanting something you can't find anywhere else, take a trek into St. Louis County and grab some dinner and drinks at Ferguson Brewing Company, my personal favorite. This cozy restaurant brews around 20 beers in house and it is fun to peek through the windows to watch the magic happen. If you're in the area, you have got to try their Irish Red, which is available all year round.

40. THE KING OF BEERS

I would lose my St. Louisian status if I spoke about St. Louis beer and didn't mention the big guy. Anheuser-Busch has been around since the 1850s and has been offering brew tours from the 1890s on. Through the years they have acquired many other brands and have grown to be an internationally recognized brand. If you're around St. Louis in the winter, you have got to come down to the brewery for a tour and to see the festive lights, widely regarded as one of the best displays in the city.

41. CHEERS!

If it's anything, St. Louis is a city that likes to have a good time. There are countless bars, each with their own style and feel. My personal favorite spot to unwind is Venice Cafe, near the famous Cherokee Street. This funky bar often has live music and is decorated in a way that can only be described as "artistic maximalist." They are one of the few cash-only places in the city, so be sure to plan accordingly (but don't worry if you forget, they have an ATM on site).

If you're wanting something a little more subdued, go on down to the Delmar Loop and stop into Eclipse, located on the roof of the Moonrise Hotel. Make your way up to the rooftop garden bar and watch the busy Loop in action while you sip on one of their signature cocktails or snack on one of their tasty small plates. This offers a great view of the city skyline and a photo-op of the Arch.

Eat Like a Local

42. ↑ ↑ ↓ ↓ ← → ← → B A
START

A popular trend to come about recently is the barcade; part bar, part adult only arcade. St. Louis has jumped on this fun idea and has several arcade bars around the area. The first I'd like to talk about is a small chain with locations in multiple states, but that doesn't make it less of a St. Louis staple. Up, Down is a full service bar (and pizza joint!) with two floors filled with old and new arcade games. If you want a little break from the screens, step out into the patio and try out the giant Jenga or Connect Four. With each game only costing a quarter, this Up, Down is a must-do for any and all game lovers.

For a more intimate vibe, drive about half an hour out the city to St. Charles and check out Two Plumbers. They're a much smaller place than Up, Down, with fewer games and drinks, but are also generally less packed. They do not have a full service bar, but rather, sell only beers and ciders brewed in house. With classic arcade games like PacMan and Galaga, Two Plumbers has a retro feel to it that is aided by the dozen pinball machines.

43. THE PUZZLE BAR

Have you ever wanted to try a board game out before you committed to buying it? Or maybe you just remember a game from your childhood but can't find it anywhere. If either of those are the case, or you just want to play some games, Pieces is the place for you. Part bar, part casual dining, all nerd heaven. Many of the items have puntastic names, and a good chunk of the menu rotates every season. The real reason to come here though, is the library of games. With more than 850 games available, there is guaranteed to be something for everyone to enjoy. If you happen to stop by on a Wednesday night, don't be afraid to join in on the weekly trivia night!

44. NIGHTS OUT

While St. Louis, like most Midwestern cities, isn't exactly known for its crazy nightlife or club scene, we do have some options for you. Many of the bars close at 1 am or earlier, leaving much to be desired if you're in the mood for a night of dancing. If that's the case, head on down to The Pepper Lounge or Europe Nightclub. Both are only open on the weekends from 10 pm-3 am, but offer the chance for lots of dancing and drinks.

Europe Nightclub is closer to, well, your standard European nightclub. They knew what they were doing when they named it. The Pepper Lounge, though, has several distinct areas, ensuring everyone in your group will find something to do that they enjoy. You can relax in the lounge or VIP areas, dance on the dancefloor, or grab some air on the patio. Whichever of these two clubs you decide to go to, be aware that they are downtown late at night. Just keep your wits around you and you'll have a great time.

45. WHAT A DRAG

One of the most inclusive and diverse areas in the city is a several block long stretch called The Grove. This area is packed with bars, clubs, restaurants, and concert venues dedicated to being a safe home for the LGBT+ community. This vibrant mile long strip hosts the city's Pride parade and festival every June, but there are many related events year long. It's not unusual to be able to go to a drag performance any night of the week, and be on the lookout for bingo nights hosted by local drag queens.

Whatever kind of nightlife you're looking for, The Grove has it and is one of the best places in the city to go for a night out.

46. CALLING ALL SPORTS FANS

One of the best places to catch a Cardinal's game (outside the stadium that is) is located just feet away from the ballgame. Ballpark Village is a collection of diverse restaurants, bars, and clubs where everyone is sure to find something for them. It's a great place to go whether you want to watch the game, grab some drinks, or dance for a while.

If the game is why you decided to come to BPV, be sure to come early so you can eat at Cardinal Nation. This restaurant has memorabilia from every era of Cardinals history on display, and upstairs is the Cardinals Hall of Fame and Museum. Just outside this eatery is the Bud Deck, a huge room with a full bar and a 40 foot tv, a great place to watch nail-biting playoffs surrounded by fans.

However, if you'd rather not spend your vacation watching baseball (you're wrong, but I'll forgive you), there are a dozen restaurants, bars, and dance clubs you can visit too. Each of these has its own style and vibe to offer. If you like country music and bull riding, PBR is the spot for you. Maybe you're more of a live music, piano bar type person, Howl at the Moon is just around the corner. Or maybe you want something beachy and retro, if that's the case, step into Shark Bar. No matter what your interests may be, BallPark Village is a one-stop-shop for you and your friends.

47. QUIKTRIP

In a book about food, it might seem odd to have a gas station featured. QuikTrip, though, is so much more than just a gas station. Yes, they can be found all over the Midwest, but they are the most popular chain around for a reason. The "usual gas station food" here is a quality far and above any other gas station food I've ever had. You can tell the food is actually fresh, which makes a huge difference.

In addition to the normal gas station grab and go food, QuikTrip has an in-house kitchen that makes food fresh and to-order. This food ranges from build-your-own nachos and pretzels to egg flatbreads, pizzas, and specialty drinks. It's the best road trip fueling spot in the Midwest, and I am always sad to learn that I have crossed out of their territory.

48. GROCERY STORES

If you're staying somewhere with a kitchen and don't want to eat out for every meal, the best place to get your groceries like a local will be one of two chains: Schnucks and Dierbergs. These two stores are both family owned and operated, and are all over the metro-area. Schnucks is the largest local chain in the area and is known as "the friendlist stores in town." Dierbergs is the slightly priciery store of the two, and also generally has a larger selection of vegan, vegetarian, and gluten free items. Both heavily feature products from local vendors, freshly packaged meals, a pharmacy, and St. Louis apparel.

49. RAVIOLI, BUT TOASTED

Toasted ravioli seems like a strange combination of words, especially for a city with so much authentic Italian food. To make it, you take a normal ravioli, coat it in seasoned bread crumbs, and deep fry it. Top it with parmesan cheese and dip it in marinara sauce and you've got yourself St. Louis' favorite appetizer. This dish, while not authentic Italian, can be found at many of the local Italian restaurants, as well as many bars in the area. It has become such a popular dish that it can also be commonly found in local grocery stores.

50. LAST, BUT ABSOLUTELY NOT LEAST

Gooey Butter cake. Possibly my favorite dessert, no, food, of all time. It's hard to describe this dish in any other way than "unintelligible food moaning." It's a fairly dense cake made from flour, eggs, powdered sugar, and, you guessed it, butter; this gives it a sort of wiggly consistency, like cheesecake. After baking, it needs to cool and add a generous amount of powdered sugar on top and it is ready to be enjoyed. This sweet and rich delicacy can be found at many local restaurants and grocery stores. It is definitely a must try on your trip to St. Louis.

BONUS TIP #1

Many popular foods today claim their origin to be the St. Louis World's Fair in 1904. How many of these actually hark back to the Fair is debatable, but that list includes the waffle cone, the hot dog, peanut butter, iced tea, cotton candy, and the club sandwich.

BONUS TIP #2

It seems that there's a festival happening every weekend somewhere in St. Louis, be sure to look it up and see if there will be any happening while you're visiting. At these festivals you will be sure to run into a stand selling deep fried everything. I truly mean everything. Sure, you'll find the usual funnel cakes and deep fried Oreos, but chances are high that they'll be featuring any number of items that you think shouldn't be deep fried. These range from sticks of butter to pancakes. Do yourself a favor, ignore how unhealthy all of that is, and try the deep fried pancake.

If you want to go to a festival but aren't so sure about those deep fried things, look up when the Festival of Nations is scheduled for that year and try to come during it! Usually the last weekend in August

Eat Like a Local

and in Tower Grove Park, it is one of my favorite things to do every year. There are booths and events featuring countries from all over the world, all with immigrants from those countries who now call St. Louis home. It's the best place to get authentic food from every culture you can think of.

BONUS TIP #3

Going through this guide, you may be thinking to yourself that you've never tried any St. Louis food. If you live in the USA, chances are that you're wrong, you have tried St. Louis food before. If you've ever been to a Panera Bread Co, congratulations! You have had St. Louis style food! Founded here in Missouri with the name St. Louis Bread Co, it is one of our proudest exports.

READ OTHER BOOKS BY CZYK PUBLISHING

Eat Like a Local United States Cities & Towns

Eat Like a Local United States

Eat Like a Local- Oklahoma: Oklahoma Food Guide

Eat Like a Local- North Carolina: North Carolina Food Guide

Eat Like a Local- New York City: New York City Food Guide

Children's Book: Charlie the Cavalier Travels the World by Lisa Rusczyk

Eat Like a Local

Follow *Eat Like a Local on* Amazon.
Join our mailing list for new books

http://bit.ly/EatLikeaLocalbooks

CZYKPublishing.com

Made in United States
Orlando, FL
18 April 2025

60594856R00046